HERITAGE TRACTION IN COLOUR

Volume One
THE CLASS 50's

Kevin Derrick

NOSTALGIA ROAD PUBLICATIONS

The **Famous Fleets** Series ™

is produced under licence by

Nostalgia Road Publications Ltd.

Unit 6, Chancel Place

Shap Road Industrial Estate, Kendal LA9 6NZ

Tel. 01539 738832 - Fax: 01539 730075

designed and published by
Trans-Pennine Publishing Ltd.
PO Box 10,
Appleby-in-Westmorland,
Cumbria, CA16 6FA
Tel. 017683 51053 Fax. 017683 53558
e-mail: admin@transpenninepublishing.co.uk

and printed by
Kent Valley Colour Printers Ltd.
Kendal, Cumbria
01539 741344

© Trans-Pennine Publishing Ltd. 2003
Photographs: Strathwood Library or as credited

Front Cover: *50037* Illustrious *is thought to be one of the last of the class to be outshopped without being refurbished at Doncaster. It is seen here in the snows of early March, 1979 and will have running trials along the ECML before its return to Laira.* Leonard Ball (D602)

Rear Cover Top: *When still working the West Coast Main Line (WCML), 432 and 435 roll off the shed at Polmadie on the 21st August 1971.* Arthur Wilson (D595)

Rear Cover Bottom: *The early years of the class are recalled, with a re-painted D400 at Woking in November 1991.* Strathwood Library Collection (D793)

Title Page: *The appeal of the Railfreight Grey livery was taken up again on 50149* Defiance *when it passed into preservation. This splendid view, two years into its new service life, was taken at an open day at Worksop on 5th September 1993 when there were just three Class 50s still active. The yellow painted nameplates were a feature of this unique engine.* Michael Hill/Strathwood Library Collection (D581)

This Page: *This view at Lancaster shows the multiple working couplings, as 50007 is paired with D400 for a working over Shap. The cast brass arrows and the two differing versions of the shed codes painted on each locomotive are fine embellishments.* Strathwood Library Collection (D586)

INTRODUCTION

If ever there was a class of diesel locomotives that seems to have stirred up the passions of railway enthusiasts more than any other, it must be the Class 50s - the subject of this colour album.

Arriving new on the scene in late-1967 and 1968, with their shiny new 'Rail Blue' livery, the 50s came just as steam was drawing to a close in the north west of England. To steam enthusiasts they appeared to spell all that was wrong with our railways, but they quickly settled down to work! They were also unique at the time when accountants were starting to make their presence clear in the railway's management, by being the first locomotives to be leased by British Railways and not purchased outright. This was surely, a sign of the ways of today, even back in 1967?

50001 *Dreadnought*: *Looking more like it is on wedding car duties with the safety ribbons, the locomotive above is, in fact ready to return to service after refurbishment at Doncaster in 1980. This work also saw a change into the large logo livery, which your author feels suited them best. This works visit lasted three months and took the use of a cross country working to get the engine back to Bristol where it returned to regular duties.* Strathwood Library Collection (D521)

From the start, the 50s were destined to be regarded as stopgap locomotives, firstly on the northern section of the West Coast Mainline between Crewe and Glasgow in the period after the end of steam. This was of course before the electrification could be completed, and their use during this period was not just on the glamour turns like the double-headed Royal Scot or Midday Scot rosters!

In fact they could also be found working from Liverpool or Manchester to Glasgow on both passenger and parcels turns. Sometimes they even found themselves working as far north as Inverness (*photos please!*). In 1974 with the electrification almost complete from Carlisle northwards, a decision was made to purchase the class from English Electric and transfer them to the Western Region.

There they would be used to accelerate the timings as journey times were not so favourable and many businessmen had started to use the M4 and the extension of the M5 into the West Country. Things did not look good for railway travel and the HSTs were still in development; so the sound of Class 50s thumping exhausts could be enjoyed on Brunel's racetrack to Bristol and over the Devon banks.

50002 *Superb:* *In the view shown below we see that inside the works at Doncaster in 1983 the refurbishing of 50002 is well advanced. The badges and nameplates have been refitted prior to any painting, but if compared with the view on page 59 we can clearly tell that the positions of these embellishments changed over the years. In fact this poses the question as to whether this move was for merely aesthetics or to deter theft of these now valuable collector's items? Upon return to traffic after this major refurbishment,* Superb *would spend the next three years in the large logo livery before being repainted into the early version of Network South East livery after yet another visit to the 'Plant' early in 1987. Note that 50002 retains its TOPS running number, albeit in chalked figures.*
Strathwood Library Collection (D522)

As BR began to deploy the HST sets on more and more services throughout the network, so the Class 50s fell back to duties on what must be regarded as secondary routes. Consequently, cross-country services and the long (almost branch-like) line that remained of the Waterloo to Exeter route became their stomping grounds. Their use on trains from Paddington for Birmingham, Cheltenham, Oxford and Worcester was the norm, although the glory days of the 'Cheltenham Flyer' were not to return even though they had the capability of 100mph running.

A masterstroke was the decision to name the class after Royal Navy warships with the first being *Ark Royal* in 1978. This gave a growing band of enthusiasts around the country something to chase after the demise of the Westerns in 1977.

50003 *Temeraire*: *The view above shows Doncaster Works, who took over the responsibility for repairs and overhauls from Crewe in 1977. In 1979 50003 was sent there for attention after collision damage at the far cab end, but this was changed to a full refurbishment instead, thus keeping* Temeraire *out of traffic for a full 18-months. Note the plating over of the head code panels and the installation of marker lights before refurbishing.* John Ferneyhaugh (D523)

Right up to their disappearance, and through the passing of that other English Electric product - the Deltics, the class held their followers. So much so that rivalries between fans of the English Electric and the Sulzer-engined locos, fuelled such friendly rivalry and banter, it was almost reminiscent of the days of steam and the Big Four!

Today we can be thankful to those who have shared their colour slides of the heyday of the class with us. Furthermore, thanks are due to the hard working people who have preserved so many of the Class 50s, for our enjoyment on the nation's preservation railways or centres, not to mention back on the mainline. Well done indeed.

Special thanks should be given for the invaluable help and assistance from Jo Burr and David Keogh from the Fifty Fund , Bryan Jones and Paul Taylor from the Renown and Repulse Restoration Group and to all those others who have proved to me conclusively that I did not know enough about Class 50s before I started this project!

I hope that you enjoy this selection of images from the Strathwood Library and that you will be moved to make contact with us, not only to buy duplicate slides to enhance your own collection, but also to possibly share with others, access to your work for their enjoyment in the future publications we have planned. We are always pleased to hear from you in this respect and would welcome requests for subjects for future volumes in the Heritage Traction series. Watch out for our advertisements for the next four volumes in 2004, as other classes get the treatment.

Kevin Derrick, Scotland.   December 2003

D404 (later 50004): *To the left we see D404 in 1969, when it was 18 months old, calling at Carlisle while working an Anglo-Scottish express north of Crewe. The 50s were taken on for accelerating the timings over the banks of Beattock and Shap as an interim measure before full electrification. The small plate denoting the leasing arrangements can be seen midway along the sides of the locomotive. As 50004 it was named* St. Vincent *on 9th May 1978, as the first 13 members of the class were all called after the Battleships of the 1914 Grand Fleet. HMS* St. Vincent *took part in the Battle of Jutland and had a service life of only 13 years before being sold for scrap on 1st December 1921. Its locomotive namesake lasted 25 years before scrapping at Booths of Rotherham in May of 1992.* Neil Snuggs (D524)

50005: *Having been D405, it has just been renumbered into the the then new TOPS system after paying a brief works visit to Crewe in August 1974; this being after the end of six and a half years in traffic on the WCML. She will most likely have a test trip to Carlisle and back, before being returned to the Western Region. At this time 50005 was allocated to Old Oak Common, but like many of the early members that were transferred to the Western Region she was first sent to Bristol Bath Road. The name of* Collingwood *also taken from one of the* St. Vincent *class of Battleships, but was not applied until April of 1978. The now redundant head code panels have yet to be plated over, so 50005 sports dots for the time being.*
John Ferneyhaugh (D525)

50006 *Neptune*: *Seen (left) waiting to depart, with the 12.25 Exeter to Waterloo from Exeter St. David's station, 50006 was the first of the class to be refurbished, returning to traffic again on 13th November 1979. She is seen on 22nd June 1981 with just less than six years more life in service. When first introduced this locomotive was used by the BR Research Department at Derby for braking trials for her first six weeks of use; she ended her life nearby at Vic Berry's yard at Leicester in March of 1988. Jim Bryant (D526)*

50007 *Hercules*: *Drowning out the sound of the adjacent Class 33, 50007 departs (top right) from Bristol on 21st April 1981. For many people it was the distinctive sound of the exhaust on these engines that attracted their enthusiastic following. The name of* Hercules *was only carried from April 1978 until February 1984, and five months of that period was spent on a refurbishment at the Doncaster Works. Therefore there are many enthusiasts that will have perhaps missed photographing her in this un-refurbished guise. No doubt they made up for that once she was turned out renamed and painted in what was a mock Great Western livery after 1984; more of this later on. Jim Bryant (D527)*

50008 *Thunderer*: *Captured under the magnificent roof of Brunel's train shed at Paddington in January of 1981, this bottom right view shows us an un-refurbished locomotive with both its nameplates and the later fitments of its badges still in original position. By this time she had been located at Laira for nearly five years, but turns on the Waterloo run also brought her to the capital via a very different route indeed.* Trevor Walton (D528)

50009 *Conqueror:* *The picture to the left shows 50009 looking like it has been reduced to a Bo-Bo (whilst on accommodation bogies), and is pictured during its refurbishment program at Doncaster Works. It was caught on film there in December 1981, but it had in fact been the first of the class to arrive at the Plant for repair on 4th January 1977. In between, the name of* Conqueror *had been bestowed on her in May of 1978. The return of this engine to service would be in the much-loved large logo livery.* Leonard Ball (D529)

50010 *Monarch:* *This locomotive became something of a celebrity, enjoying a blue roof during the time it was in the large logo livery. This paint scheme was applied after a light repair at Landore and was popular among enthusiasts, as light grey or black roofs were usually the norm. We see her above at Bristol Temple Meads on the 09.25 Cardiff to Weymouth on 18th August 1984. She would be called to Doncaster for an intermediate overhaul just seven months later.* Jim Bryant (D530)

D411 (later 50011): *In this picture dating from August 1968 (top left) we are somewhat off the beaten track for Class 50s. Taken when steam had just finished in her native north west, the loco had been sent for tyre turning at Toton Depot when just five months old. This work was required, as it seems some drivers had been a little harsh in applying the brakes as they were getting used to 50s after the very different characteristics of Class 40s. This locomotive was the last to be named when, exactly 11 years later the name of* Centurian *was applied. With a working life of 19 years 11 months on the mainline it was the shortest lived in service. However it lingered on at Crewe Works as a test bed for another five years before being cut up on site by Texas Metals in September 1992.*
Michael Beeton (D531)

50012 *Benbow:* *The next class member (seen bottom left) appears to be too loud for the ears of this young man on Salisbury station on 15th May 1982, or perhaps he prefers the sounds of Sulzer engines in some Class 33s nearby.* Benbow *was a name given previously to the Swindon-built Warship Class locomotive D805, which also worked on the Exeter to Waterloo line until 1973. This Class 50 managed to fall into the turntable pit at Old Oak Common in January 1988 and although repaired at Laira, it succumbed to withdrawal a year later and had been completely cut up by Vic Berry's scrapmen at Leicester by May 1989.*
Strathwood Library Collection (D532)

50013 *Agincourt*: *After the disgrace of failing at Paddington on 16th May 1979, 50013 (top right) is being hauled off to Old Oak Common by 47480 for an investigation as to the cause. Seen seven months away from her refurbishment, she has been carrying that evocative name since April 1978. Interestingly the vessel* HMS Agincourt, *after whom she was named, was originally going to be called* Sultan Osman I *as it was to be commissioned for the Turkish Navy. However when World War I broke out Winston Churchill had it delivered from Armstrong's yard as* HMS Agincourt *(earning the nickname the Gin Palace) to His Majesty's Royal Navy. The Battleship lasted just seven years in the fleet before scrapping in 1922. It was not a fortunate name for the locomotive either, as fire damage led to her being withdrawn in March 1988 before going to her fate at Vic Berry's yard in 1989.*
Steven Feltham(D533)

50014 *Warspite*: *Staying at Paddington in May 1979 (with our botton right picture), we see the last of the class to be refurbished. This locomotive arrived at Doncaster for this work in May 1983 and was returned to traffic in December 1983. Exactly four years later, in December 1987, 50014 was switched off for the last time before becoming yet another victim to the torches of that famous yard in Leicester in May 1989. This was the first of three Class 50 engines in a row to pick up names from the* Queen Elizabeth *class of Battleships.*
Strathwood Library Collection (D534)

50015 *Valiant*: *Here* Valiant *is the subject of our attentions (above) at Newton Abbott in 1979. This is thought to be the first of the class to venture onto the Southern Region, as it was seen at Clapham Junction after working milk from Cornwall in November 1974!*

The 50s were to become an everyday sight on the Southern for the next nine years, with the last runs being on the Exeter trains, which in turn brought out crowds of photographers in their final months.
Leonard Ball (D535)

50016 *Barham:* *The effects of the weather, daily traffic and limited cleaning were very clear to see on the paintwork of British Rail locomotives in the 1970s and '80s. This is well illustrated (below) on 50016, when photographed at Reading in the late winter of 1982, despite the fact that the locomotive has not been back in service for many weeks after refurbishment. In selecting material for this book it seems that every shot we could find of the class in snow, shows them without snow ploughs fitted, and of course in those shots where the ploughs are fitted and ready, there is not a snowflake in sight!*
Strathwood Library Collection (D536)

50017 *Royal Oak:* *Working into Gloucester with a Cheltenham train just days after release from refurbishment, we see 50017 (above) in February 1980. The early-refurbished locomotives went back into use with the new headlamp mountings plated over, as the lamps were not ready. The* Royal Oak *name had been used before on the Class 43 North British-built Warship D842. Although commemorating one of the R Class Battleships from the 20th century, it is a name that has seen repeated use over centuries by the Royal Navy.* Trevor Walton (D537)

50018 *Resolution:* *Snaking a load of just seven coaches over the complicated point-work leading into Paddington early in 1983, 50018 (right) is fresh from Doncaster. It can be assumed the two enthusiasts leaning out in the first coach have enjoyed a lively run from Reading. The build up from the exhaust ports on the grey roof panels can also be clearly seen, and this in turn led to the depots painting the roof panels in black as a means of trying to keep up appearances.*
Strathwood Library Collection (D538)

D419 (later 50019): *Fresh from the Vulcan Foundry works of English Electric at Newton-le-Willows, D419 is seen above just after her arrival at Crewe Works on 7th April 1968. It would be another 20 days before she was officially allocated to service on the LNWL code to be changed shortly after to D05, which was the Stoke Division; even though all maintenance was carried out at Crewe Diesel Depot and certainly not Cockshute, which was Stoke's depot/stabling point. The name* Ramilies *was applied ten years later in April 1978, and this was once again yet another name that had previously been applied to both a Ship Of The Line and a Class 43 locomotive (D837).*
Michael Patterson (D539)

50020 *Revenge:* *Found at Eastleigh with a diverted 08.13 Exeter to Waterloo service, 50020 is pictured (top right) during a brief flurry of snow on 16th March 1985. Another five years of active service were left for this locomotive on the Southern and Western main lines before she went north to Rotherham and into Booths scrapyard, to be gone forever by May 1992.*
Martin Hubbard (D540)

50021 *Rodney:* *Rolling gently up to couple on to her (or should it be his) train, Rodney is seen bottom right in this pleasing study at Paddington in May 1982. The opaque marker lights in the head code panel show up well in this view, which was taken just a month on from the locomotive's release from Doncaster Works.*
Strathwood Library Collection (D541)

D422 (later 50022): *By 30th March 1969 all the Class 50s had entered service, mostly on main passenger duties, but it was a long time before there were any thoughts towards naming them. In fact, at their introduction, there were no intentions of even taking the locos into capital stock. The view below shows the locomotive that would eventually become 50022 Anson, along with other members of the class (430, 407 and 410) at Crewe North stabling point.*

This is all that was left of Crewe North sheds, the original 5A shed code, which closed officially on the 24th June 1965. Locomotives continued to be stabled here until 1970, but often run up to sleepers placed crudely as stops at the ends of the tracks. It can be seen that the mountings for the multiple working jumper cables are all still blanked off. Sadly this was another Class 50 to meet its end at Vic Berry's.
Frank Hornby (D542)

50023 *Howe*: *The locomotive seen above found fame as the first of the class to go into the large logo livery, when it emerged from Doncaster in August 1980. At first this was not necessarily a popular livery with everyone, but it quickly found favour with spotters as it made it so much easier to identify locos at speed or at a distance. At first,* Howe *was noted on test without a logo at all and with only small numerals*

Still looking respectable nearly two years later, it has command of the 15.25 Exeter to Waterloo on 20th June 1982. Howe *along with 50017* Royal Oak *were the first pair of locomotives to display Network South East livery in June 1986. Unfortunately, Booths of Rotherham took delivery of the locomotive for scrapping in 1990.*
Ian Beckey (D543)

21

50024 *Vanguard*: *Showing the later changes to the large logo and black roof panels, 50024 (top left) also has the additional orange cant rail relief lining to help warn against overhead wires. To this writer, it seems to make the locomotives look less attractive, even when running alongside the sea wall near Dawlish in July 1987. It should also be noted that the buffer beam is now red in this view - another subtlety, as some were still black in this scheme. After withdrawal, Coopers Metals cut the engine up at Old Oak Common depot in September 1991.* Strathwood Library Collection (D544)

50025 *Invincible*: *At journey's end on the buffers at Paddington (bottom left), the glow of the 50025's red tail lamp shines bright, as does the 1950s vintage oil lamp on the platform. The commemorative plates fixed above the engine's nameplates were presented by the ship's company of HMS* Invincible *and were sadly only carried for a short while. In 1989 Vic Berry's men scrapped this locomotive, as they did with several other members of the class, but unusually they did so at Old Oak Common depot and not their Leicester scrapyard; see the picture on page 45.* Strathwood Library Collection (D545)

50026 *Indomitable*: *Showing the image that was created by the first version of Network South East livery, 50026 is seen below with a rake of MkI and MkII coaches on an Oxford working at White Waltham in this May 1988 view; the crop of oil seed rape growing in the field alongside adds a splash of even more colour* to the scene. *Named after the* Invincible *Class battleship launched in March 1907 and sold out of service in 1922, this Class 50 is one of many to see further service after being sold into preservation at the end of her working life.*
Strathwood Library Collection (D546)

50027 Lion: *The Network South East livery was revised again in the summer of 1987, but to many enthusiasts this was 'no improvement at all!' A rather shabby looking Lion is seen above, waiting to run the stock for another Exeter working down to Waterloo in January of 1990, and is viewed from the footbridge that spanned all of the sidings at Clapham Junction. HMS Lion was a World War I battle-cruiser and like many things that are neither one thing nor the other, it was not a success, despite this dubious claim to fame the locomotive lives on in preservation!* (D547 Strathwood Library Collection)

50028 *Tiger: While performing a light engine movement at Birmingham New Street in 1983, 50028 seems to have drawn a small gathering of spotters. By this time the class were finding favour on cross-country workings to Bristol and the southwest. Even with another eight years of service left, the class had their devotees with many enthusiasts travelling far and wide to enjoy Class 50 haulage. This is one species of Tiger that became extinct due to the activities of Coopers Metals at Old Oak Common in October 1991. (D548 Strathwood Library Collection)*

50029 *Renown*: *By December 1991* Renown *has just over a year to run before being taken out of traffic, but in this view (top left) it burbles away in a wintry scene at Waterloo. As part of the changes involved in both versions of the Network South East livery, the nameplates were moved higher up the locomotive's side.* Strathwood Library Collection(D549)

50030 *Repulse*: *Waterloo was a good place to find Class 50 activity towards the end and we return there once again in December 1990. In this (bottom left) view* Repulse *has a rake of TC stock in tow, but how the mighty have fallen! HMS* Repulse *was a World War I battle-cruiser who by World War II was finding it hard to keep up and was sadly sunk by the Japanese along with HMS* Prince of Wales *in December 1941. In complete contrast the locomotive carrying the ship's name was preserved for the future by the same group of enthusiasts who saved sister locomotive 50029* Renown. Strathwood Library Collection (D550)

50031 *Hood*: *The pride of the Royal Navy, HMS* Hood *was tragically lost in an epic engagement with the German Battleship* Bismarck *in May 1941. After its naming as* Hood, *this Class 50 took a special place in the hearts of many and in April 1983 it received twinning plates from the Class 50 Locomotive Group. Seen right, and in a very well turned out large logo livery it has the small Network South East chevron logos affixed to the head code boxes. Without doubt, she outshines her train easily on the ex-LSWR mainline near Farnborough in 1988. The locomotive passed into preservation after coming out of service in August 1991.* Strathwood Library Collection (D551)

D432 (later 50032): *The view below brings us back to the early days of the class on the WMCL, this time to Crewe South 5B. Just like Crewe North it continued to be used for stabling locomotives after official closure on 6th November 1967. However as can be seen here in this view taken in July 1968, the new (and very clean) D432 from Vulcan Foundry, alongside a pair of work-weary ten-year-old class 24s has yet to enter traffic. Later to be named* Courageous *and carrying black-painted nameplates after a repaint into Network South East livery. She was not one to reach the safety of preservation, being scrapped by Coopers Metals at Old Oak Common in April 1991.*

Ironically, by lasting to the end of its working life, the locomotive fared somewhat better than the Royal Navy vessel that it was named after. As a matter of record HMS Courageous *was launched on 5th February 1916 and commissioned in January 1917. It was then converted into an aircraft carrier between June 1924 and May 1928, but was sadly the first major loss of a British warship during World War II. That conflict was just a couple of weeks old when the carrier was torpedoed by the German submarine U29 in the Irish Sea on 17th September 1939.*
Strathwood Library Collection (D552)

50033 *Glorious*: *Destined to become another celebrity locomotive, 50039 is seen pictured above fully dressed in her Network South East livery with absolutely everything bulled up, even the snow ploughs. The positioning of the nameplate to read 'Glorious Network South East' is clear in this view taken at Reading in February 1990. The locomotive passed to the National Railway Museum at the end of its active service life in March 1994.*
Strathwood Library Collection (D553)

50034 *Furious*: *Seen above in the splendid surroundings of Paddington, 50034 is wearing the early Network South East paint scheme. By this stage (April 1987) Class 50 workings into Paddington were becoming less and less frequent, although the Newbury or Oxford trains could still turn up behind a 50. This was yet another locomotive to face the oxy-acetylene torches of Coopers Metals at Old Oak Common in April 1991.*
Strathwood Library Collection (D554)

50035: *Captured during that short period when the renumbered Class 50s were still at work on the WCML north of Crewe in September 1974, the view of 50035 (below) was taken at Wigan North Western. As* Ark Royal *it was to become the first of the class to be named in January 1978 with the crests being fitted shortly afterwards; these are shown in detail towards the back of the book. The class became another firm favourite because of the positive naming policy to commemorate other warships, so with* Ark Royal *having been a traditional flagship name it was fitting that the 50s should start here.*

Perhaps this connection was more appropriate, when the naming ceremony was at Laira depot in Plymouth, a city with historic naval traditions. It should also be noted that many locomotives of this time ran with their new numbers and the Inter City arrows at both ends of the engine. Once it was decided to have only one number on each side of the locomotive, many an enthusiast either missed numbers at speed, or had their photograph impaired by catching their shot with the numbered end at the rear.

Leonard Ball (D555)

50036 *Victorious*: Once again we pick on a Class 50 with a warship name that had previously been used on a Class 43 D860. However, before the diesels, it should be remembered that many of these splendid warship names were first used for the naming of several of Sir William Stanier's Jubilee 4-6-0s. Now once again we have snowploughs in this view, but there is no promise of snow under Paddington's roof as it is August 1990!

However, you will note that the engine above has a red buffer beam together with the Network South East chevron markings on the head code panels. It is almost the end for 50036 for in seven months she will be withdrawn before ending her days at the hands of Booths of Rotherham in the summer of 1992. I wonder if they removed the snowploughs first?
Strathwood Library Collection (D556)

50037 *Illustrious*: As if to prove the point about snow we have this lovely winter scene at Lavington near Westbury on 17th January 1978, even though it has not fallen deep enough to be regarded as the wrong or even the right kind of snow! What is of note again in this case, is the use of Inter City arrows placed amidships where the nameplate will be fitted in July of that year (as seen on the front cover). After withdrawal from service *Illustrious* migrated back to Glasgow in January of 1993, this time to be dismantled by M.C. Metal Processing.

Roger Griffiths (D557)

D438 (later 50038): *Coupled and running in multiple with 410, the pair are shown above whilst passing through Kilmarnock on 11th September 1971. Furthermore, they are somewhat off their usual route for a Euston to Glasgow service, but you can almost hear the exhausts as the pair head north once again. Although not in the same class as the electrics used on the grades of Shap and Beattock today, the sound was certainly to be enjoyed by enthusiasts with the windows open, even if it did upset some of the other passengers with the fumes drifting back!*

The nameplate Formidable *was applied in May 1978, to commemorate the warship of the same name. It is interesting to record that this particular engine managed to have at least three accidents of some note in her service life. Even so, Vic Berry's men finished her off at Old Common in August 1989.*
Arthur Wilson (D558)

50039 *Implacable*: *In what was the home for many of the class, 50039 is found at Old Oak Common; yet for some this was their graveyard as well with nine of them being cut up on site. Already withdrawn from service three months earlier, the headlamps have been removed as spares in this scene (top right) at Old Oak Common in September 1989.* Implacable *would linger around the shed yards for another two years before Coopers Metals reduced her to a pile of easily removable scrap!* Strathwood Library Collection (D559)

440 (later 50044): *Remarkably although the renumbering process was already under way, Crewe Works still turned out this engine as 440 after its overhaul on 19th August 1973 (bottom left). It appears that 50036 was to be the first so treated in October of that year with the last (50005) being done by August 1974. This was first of all matched with the name* Leviathan *on 15th August 1981 only to be renamed* Centurian *in July 1987 after 50011* Centurion *was withdrawn. Interestingly it poses a question as whether or not somebody had been doing their homework for the naming. In fact HMS* Centurian *was a 'masquerade battleship', after being converted from the Canadian Pacific liner* Tyrolia. *With the careful use of mock turrets, guns and other devices fashioned from wood and canvas, and ballasted to look just like the real thing, it was designed to confuse the enemy! Whereas HMS* Centurion *was indeed a pre-Dreadnought Battleship of the Royal Navy. But why pick on* Leviathan *for removal of the name, as she was a Drake Class Armoured Cruiser with World War I service?* Frank Hornby (D560)

50041 *Bulwark*: *Seen above at Paddington in October 1982, and with a very light load indeed, is another famous member of the class; but famous for all the wrong reasons as 50041 was involved in the dramatic crash at Paddington on 23rd November 1983. Whilst bringing the night sleeper from Penzance in to Paddington far too fast, 50041 rolled over on her side and crashed under a substantial girder bridge. Thank heavens it was not a repeat of the Lewisham disaster of December 1957 and the bridge held firm. Perhaps it was because 50041 was only two years out from a full refurbishment at the time of the derailment, that resources were eventually made available to repair her. After another six years of service the repaired locomotive finally fell prey to Coopers Metals at Old Oak Common.*
Strathwood Library Collection (D561)

50042 *Triumph*: *Showing off to good effect, the addition of a roof painted dark grey (but without the use of an orange cant rail warning lining) is 50042 in the large logo livery. Seen below on Saturday 11th August 1984 it stands at Platform 3 of Bristol's Temple Meads station with the 07.40 Penzance to Glasgow, which it will take as far as Birmingham New Street. The naming of the locomotive as* Triumph *commemorates* HMS Triumph *a member of the* Swiftsure *class of battleships, which was launched in 1903.*

The name Triumph *had been used on a diesel locomotive before (D855, a North British-built Class 43), but that one was actually named after a 1946-commissioned aircraft carrier. Interestingly the Royal Navy has had several vessels of the same name, including a submarine from 1939 (lost off Greece in 1942) and today's* Trafalgar *class submarine HMS* Triumph, *which has Tomahawk capability. Perhaps, one day in the future some other British locomotive will be bestowed with this illustrious naval name.* Ian Beckey (D562)

50043 Eagle: *Taking a little time out (top left), Eagle is on the stabling point at Oxford on 8th February 1984 while some of the class were being used on the Oxford to Paddington turns.*
Strathwood Library Collection (D563)

50044 Exeter: *Shown (bottom left) most appropriately at Exeter St. David's, 50044 has just brought in the 07.40 from Bristol Temple Meads on 20th June 1982. Fresh from Doncaster and proudly displaying the twinning plates above the nameplates, it is easy to see why many enthusiasts favoured this colour scheme.*
Ian Beckey (D564)

50045 *Achilles: Returning once again to Exeter, this time during August 1986, we see (above) the Class 50 member that was named after the famous HMS* Achilles. *Along with HM ships* Exeter *and* Ajax, Achilles *was one of the three cruisers that had the task of forcing the German pocket battleship* Graf Spee *to run for cover in Montevideo harbour after the Battle of the River Plate in 1939, where she scuppered herself rather than face all the other British warships it believed were steaming hard down the South Atlantic for the kill. It was certainly a popular decision to name link the class to these wonderful names from British naval history. It is a pity that she went to Booths of Rotherham at the end of her service days.*
Strathwood Library Collection (D565)

50046 *Ajax: The last of the trio of Class 50 locomotives named after the famous River Plate warriors is also caught at Exeter St. David's in September 1991 (left), this time displaying the addition of the orange warning line around the roof. Once again this was to be an unfortunate engine and missed preservation in March the following year after her withdrawal. Instead M.C. Metals in Glasgow claimed 50046 and she was cleanly dispatched by June of 1992.*
Strathwood Library Collection (D566)

50047: *Racing past Blatchbridge Junction with another service for the West Country we see 50047 in March 1977 (top right). This was at a time well before the class felt the full effects of the HSTs stealing their duties from the timetables. She was to later carry the name* Swiftsure *for almost ten years until she became one of the earlier withdrawals and was consigned to Vic Berry in Leicester who had completed her disposal by July 1989.*
Roger Griffiths (D567)

50048 *Dauntless: Arriving at Paddington at a respectable speed,* Dauntless *is seen (bottom right) on 14th May 1983. By this stage the allocation of the Class 50s was split between Laira and Old Oak Common, even so it was still possible to see maintenance being carried out at Bath Road and even Landore from time to time. While trips back to Doncaster for casual maintenance were still taking place into the late 1980s. Ultimately,* Dauntless *joined four other class members by ending her days north of the border at M.C. Metals in Glasgow during 1992.*
Strathwood Library Collection (D568)

50049 Defiance: *Although it was the last of the 50-strong class to be delivered from English Electric, going into service on 11th December 1968, 50049 acquired celebrity status as a result of being selected for trials as a sub class of 50/1. In these it was altered internally to be better equipped for handling freight trains in the summer of 1987. From an enthusiast's viewpoint this meant not only another renumbering to 50149, but a change of livery (seen at the front of the book) into Railfreight Grey, but it is here captured in Network South East colours!*

Perhaps more importantly it was seen as a possible reprieve for the class, for if this was a success they could have been found use elsewhere on the network. This was not to be the case as can be seen from the above view at Clapham Junction in February 1992, when Defiance *succumbed to the final livery variation for the class in service, namely the later version of Network South East livery. Her days as 50149 are fondly remembered by somebody, with the unofficial extra numbers (149) on the front of the locomotive.* Strathwood Library Collection (D569)

400 (later 50050): *It is 14th August 1972 and the spotter's grapevine is alive to the fact that there is the first Class 50 on Bath Road seen below. This was five years after English Electric built D400 at Vulcan Foundry, although it was not until September of 1967 that she ventured out onto the mainline under test. But here we are at a time when consideration is being made to use the class again as a stopgap, and to speed up the timings on the Western Region before the HST deliveries. So as they had done on the WCML before electrification, they would do it again.*

However they were sadly not to be used double-headed on the Devon Banks as they had been on the steep ascents over Shap and Beattock, which were encountered between Lancaster and Glasgow. It would be renumbered as 50050, because the TOPS system could not cope with 50000, and from 1978 it was given the name Fearless. *Later still it was decided to repaint her back into the original livery for the class to achieve more enthusiast revenue. By then the accountants were starting to make the decisions as well!*

Roger Griffiths (D570)

THE CRASH VICTIMS

The first member of the Class 50s was DP2, or as it was officially classed, Diesel Prototype Two. Using a spare Deltic body shell, the project was developed to attract additional business to English Electric, as there was some resistance to the Napier Deltic engines, even though the need for 100mph capability was an obvious attraction. This apparently luckless prototype should however be regarded as a success, in more ways than one.

Not only did it act as a superb sales and development tool for English Electric from 1962, bringing us the Class 50s, but also because the Portuguese took up on the development of the engines for valuable export orders for their railways as well. Tragically the locomotive DP2 was to be virtually destroyed when it crashed at Thirsk on 31st July 1967, just days before D400 was completed. It returned to Vulcan Foundry and was cut up in 1968, although it is suggested that the engines were swapped from DP2 to D400 in May 1968.

DP2: *Colour photographs of accident victims are extremely thin on the ground as my editor, the author of the* Trains In Trouble *series, keeps telling me. Although he has pictures of the DP2 incident in black and white, he does not have any in colour, as a result we portray DP2 (left) on display at Marylebone in its revised two-tone green livery. It is said that originally there were plans to paint D400 in green and not blue, and that it may indeed have happened in the works. Similar legends exist over Swindon Works painting a Western black in the early 1960s to see what it looked like; and this may be possible, after all Crewe was still turning out new Class 47s in green in 1967!*
Bob Treacher/Alton Model Centre (D571)

50025 *Invincible*: *Ironically, despite its strong-sounding name, this was the only member of the entire class to be withdrawn as a direct result of crash or accident damage. After a mishap at West Ealing it was withdrawn almost straightaway in August of 1989 and was removed to Old Oak Common where Vic Berry's team of mobile cutters had finished her off by October. We can survey the damage here (bottom left) in this September 1989 view and wonder if the policy for phasing out the class had not already been taken at that point in time; for if not wouldn't she have simply been sent back to the Doncaster Works for repairs?*
Strathwood Library Collection (D572)

THE NAME CHANGES

As mentioned in the text, the class were originally put into traffic without names, but this omission was later rectified by the British Railways Board who realised that there was 'mileage' (good public relation value) to be obtained from naming locomotives. Even so the names were not always for life, and we see here a couple of before and after examples of name changes that subsequently took place.

50040 *Leviathan: Seen (above) at Reading in December 1982, 50040 carried this name from 15th September 1981 until July 1987.* Strathwood Library Collection (D573)

50040 *Centurian: After 5th July 1987 and until she was withdrawn in August 1990, 50040 appeared with a name change and this spelling. It is seen right on 1st November 1988 at Didcot Parkway while engaged in the 17.32 Paddington to Oxford.* David Keogh (D574)

50007 Hercules: *From 6th April 1980 and referred to by many as 'Edward The Green Engine' (as she became nicknamed) after the* Sir Edward Elgar *plates were fitted to 50007 on 25th February 1984. Caught at Oxford, when not long back from Doncaster in March 1983, it is seen left in the popular large logo livery.*
Strathwood Library Collection (D575)

50007 Sir Edward Elgar: *It is interesting that the name change for 50007 should be part of the Great Western 150 celebrations for 1985, as the selected Class 47s received names firmly associated with the Great Western Railway. The musician Edward Elgar had no notable railway associations, although he was born in GWR territory (Worcester) in 1857.*

Until the outstanding success of the Enigma Variations in 1899, he was considered a 'provincial' composer; and a largely self-taught one at that! Although his name was also carried by the Castle Class 4-6-0 7005 and even earlier by Bulldog 4-4-0 3414, why (if names of a railway nature were being chosen) the name of Sir James Milne or perhaps Swindon were not used? But then again as Swindon Works was to close at this time, we could ask was this an act of political cowardice? Although the name change and green livery were not liked by everyone, 50007 did become the star attraction of countless open days and special workings. We see the engine (above) at Paddington on a regular service train for Birmingham in December 1985, with the silver buffers still evident from a summer of open day appearances.
Strathwood Library Collection (D576)

THE CLASS 50 VARIATIONS

Like Elgar had his variations, so too the Class 50s had theirs and as already seen from some of the views, many subtle and different liveries or details have been tried from time to time; a few of these are presented here to represent the changes, but this is by no means a complete review.

50023 *Howe*: *Above we see the black window surrounds, which gave an almost highwayman appearance to the earlier Network South East livery as exampled in the view above at Oxford in May 1989.* Strathwood Library Collection (D577)

50024 *Vanguard*: *Buffer beams on most of the class have tended to be painted in black or at least with all the muck thrown up they always appeared to be that way. However one or two seem to have picked up an enthusiastic localised repaint in this area, perhaps as a result of minor repairs. Whatever, it certainly helps to bring some cheer to this freezing scene at Waterloo during the freeze of March 1987 as* Vanguard *(seen right) cuddles up with a Class 73 and a Class 33 (both just out of the picture) to help keep warm!*
Strathwood Library Collection (D578)

50028 *Tiger: A similar livery treatment to that shown on the previous page has been applied here on this later version of Network South East livery to Tiger. It is seen above at Clapham Junction in November 1990, just three months before coming out of service. Also to be seen is the pod for the driver's radio telephone equipment, which was fitted towards the end of the 1980s on top of the headcode boxes.*
Strathwood Library Collection (D579)

50035 Ark Royal: *Perhaps the most interesting variation of all was that carried by Ark Royal, which is seen (right) at Birmingham New Street on Tuesday 15th July 1986. This was just after the launch of the Network South East livery, and at a time when Doncaster Works did not have the 'painting by numbers' for the new livery pattern. A decision was made to send the ex-works locomotive down to Bristol on a cross-country working, and Ark Royal was then hidden in Bath Road depot until nightfall and was run light engine to Old Oak Common for painting that evening. A real rarity indeed, notice the black numbers half way along the engine sides!* David Keogh (D580)

50015 *Valiant*: *Although painted for active service it is perhaps inevitable that this locomotive should enjoy celebrity status too, once it was painted into the 'Dutch' livery. Seen here (above) at Hereford Rail Day on 5th May 1991, it has another year in service before preservation. Once again the use of snowploughs are more of a fashion accessory, as it surely will not snow in Hereford in May! Notice should also be given to the use of dark grey on the bogies and running gear. Compared with Defiance you can make your own decisions as to which is the ugly duckling?* Ian Beckey (D582)

50008 *Thunderer*: *Several versions of the 'Engineers Blue' livery were tried on the class and perhaps the most attractive was that applied to* Thunderer, *which is pictured above when coupled to* Valiant *for a special working at Penzance in 1991. This notoriety and a longer service career have once again helped another 'Hoover' into the safety of preservation. This vacuum cleaner nickname seems to have stuck to the Class 50s, although your author has never quite managed to find a domestic appliance yet with quite the same sound!*
Strathwood Library Collection (D583)

50019 *Ramilies*: *Although an oddball repaint into 'Engineers Blue', this locomotive did not enjoy as much of the limelight as its contemporaries. Captured here (above) at Bristol Temple Meads, it is waiting to work the 19.54 Cardiff to Southampton general parcels on 1st August 1990, when it has just another month in traffic. Again enough extra time was bought to allow for her preservation. Note the yellow chevron markings at the far cab and the use of larger numerals.* Ian Beckey (D584)

50004 *St. Vincent*: *In the first of two further night-time views by Bristol-based photographers, we see 50004 (top right) posed with its cab lights on at Bath Road on 5th January 1990, with a grey roof once again.* Jim Bryant (D596)

50037 *Illustrious*: *This locomotive was to be less fortunate among the celebrities in 'Engineers Blue' as she was not saved. However we can remember the engine from this pleasant view at Bristol (bottom right), with the 21.45 Temple Meads to Southampton parcels on 9th March 1990. Once again larger numerals are used, whilst larger Inter City arrows and an odd nameplate position are evident.* Ian Beckey (D585)

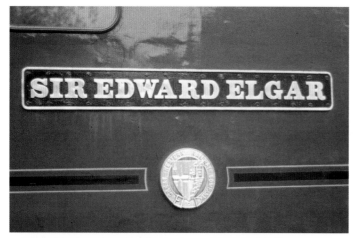

In these pages we take a look at some of the nameplates, crests and badges that have adorned Class 50 locomotives from time to time. We start with 50007, which we saw in its BR Brunswick Green livery on page 2 of this book. This scheme was applied for GWR 150 celebrations, and replaced the name *Hercules*. For an older generation the livery change and cast number plates were a trip down memory lane, for a younger generation it often meant something else. Yet from a public relations point of view, the re-naming and livery changes were a great success even if the name was not quite as appropriate as it could have been.

50007 *Sir Edward Elgar*: *The nameplates and badges fitted to this locomotive (top left) were in keeping with the other Great Western 150 locomotives, with a tasteful application of lining in the traditional Swindon manner. One does wonder how the Class 50s might have looked had they been painted in a scheme similar to DP2 after all?*
John Williamson (D589)

50007 *Sir Edward Elgar*: *Unlike steam locomotives, which had a defined front end, diesel classes like the 50s had driving positions at either end and thus no clearly obvious end on which to position the plate. Rather than show the TOPS number at both ends, BR chose to use one end to carry the BR 'double arrow' logo appropriately finished in brass; this is well shown in the aforementioned page 2 picture. The cab at the other end of Sir Edward Elgar shows another influence from the GWR's past, this time (bottom left) with the use of a cast brass number plate. The Mayflower denotes that this locomotive was allocated to Laira depot, who were indeed very proud of their 'special' engine. This can be seen here, where another version of the shed coding has been applied, whilst a little hand-painting around the data panel has been used to hide the lack of green backed stickers!*
Strathwood Library Collection (D587)

Of course, 50007 was unique in its green livery and cast number plates etc., but the other members of the class all had their distinctive embellishments. The nameplates were relatively simple oblongs, but this tended to accentuate the more ornate crests that were variously positioned above or below the nameplates. The crests were those worn by the ship whose name the locomotive had assumed and they were therefore adorned with a royal crown.

50035 _Ark Royal_: _All is clearly not well aboard the 'Ark' as we can tell from the patterns the oil is making along the side of 50035 (top right). Unfortunately crests and twinning plates were not fitted to all of the class, as they certainly enhanced the appearance and endeared the class to many._
Leonard Ball (D590)

50031 _Hood_: _In contrast to what is said above, this plaque (centre right) is not actually an official crest received from the Royal Navy but a twinning badge presented by the Class 50 Locomotive Group._
Ian Beckey (D591)

50002 _Superb_: _Showing not only the tendency to detail the badges later on (bottom right), but also how the positioning of nameplates and badges varied over the years. This view should serve as a warning to railway modellers re-creating members of the class that they should really check prototypical photographs very carefully if they want to be strictly correct._
Strathwood Library Collection (D592)

And Finally: *The sad line up above is seen at Plymouth on 20th October 1990, with eight of the class withdrawn, and nearly all of them destined to go for scrap. It should be noticed they did not all succumb to the Network South East liveries, and many of the large logo engines had their roofs returned to the lighter grey towards the end.* Peter Salmon (D593)

We hope you have enjoyed this look back to Heritage Traction Class 50s and will join us again in future volumes. However, can we offer a reminder that all of these published shots are available to purchase as superb duplicate slide copies direct from Strathwood. The code number at the end of each slide indicates its catalogue number, and also the name of the photographer whose work we felt warranted inclusion.

To get your copy of the extensive catalogue listing of these and many thousands of other shots available in fabulous colour, please send £5.00 to: -

    Strathwood Limited
    Kirkland House
    Bruce Street, Whithorn.
    Dumfries & Galloway DG8 8PY

Or visit the websites: -

www.strathwood.com or www.railwayslide.co.uk.

In return we will send the collector's catalogue, complete with sample slide, post free to UK addresses (overseas add £2.50).